Poems for Christians

In Christ We Live – In Christ We Die

by Kenzo Amariyo

Copyright © 2022 Kenzo Amariyo PhD (AM)

All rights reserved.

No part of this publication may be reproduced, distributed, or transmitted in any form or by any means, including photocopying, recording, or any electronic or mechanical methods, without the prior written permission of the named publisher or author. Exceptions are in the case of brief quotations embodied in reviews and certain other noncommercial uses permitted by copyright law.

1st Print 2019

2nd Print 2022

Tenshi Publishing

Tiverton, Devon UK

Contact: bookpublisher@tenshipublishing.com

Paperback: ISBN-13: 978-1-7399170-6-7
E-Book: ISBN-13: 978-1-7399170-7-4

Cover Designed by **'GetCovers'**

I would like to dedicate this book to all my spiritual teachers, your teachings were and continue to be a precious gift that I will carry with me forever. I am what I am today because of your wisdom, guidance, and patience, and for that I will be eternally grateful.

Preface

Poems for Christians has been written not just to offer support upon your path, but it is also written to encourage you to think about how you live your life and Christian walk.

God means many things to many people, and even as Christians we can think very differently to one-another; especially if that other is from a different church or different denomination.

The idea of who and what God is and what that means for us all is a personal experience, and our daily walk with God can differ significantly.

Religion has the capacity to bring people together or cause a divide; it can

Preface

drive people to love and drive them to kill. But God didn't create religion and God would not want a divide and that is why God created an opportunity and a blueprint on how to live as a Holy person – Christ.

If we all worked on ourselves to develop our divine potential what a difference it would make in the world. What a light we would shine for others to see and follow.

No matter what you believe or which church you belong to, one thing that we all share is the choice to change our own life, the choice to change how we think, feel, act, and speak. We are all equal and all able to be more like Christ if that is what we truly desire.

How many times have we read or heard about the minister, (minister being used in a broad context) falling into sin, either falling into adultery, robbing the church, or luring in children? It is not ok, it is not acceptable to me, it is probably not acceptable to you, and it is certainly not

Preface

acceptable to God.

I must ask myself – *"If we truly believe in God, in Christ, in the Holy Spirit, if we are truly walking in close relationship with God, can we really commit such abominations?"* I personally do not believe so. I do not believe that if we are walking closely to *The Divine*, that *Divine Spark of Creation*, call it what you may, that we would commit such sin. We all fall short of His glory, but if we are close to God and *'hearing His voice'* and especially at the level of a minister (which does not excuse everyone else's sin) would we not hear Him telling us not to do such things?

I feel if we are truly close to God, to our Lord, to Spirit, we would feel, if not hear that still inner voice saying *'Stop.'* If our hearts are truly for that which we confess to believe in, we would heed that still inner voice.

I believe the time has come for us all to stop blaming the devil and accept responsibility for all we think, feel, speak, and do. Have you noticed we never blame

Preface

the devil for the good things we do, we take credit for that, but if it is something bad – *"the devil made me do it!!"*

But as I write this, I do not write it to bring judgement upon anyone, we all make mistakes and sin is sin whether big or small. I write this merely as a reminder, I hold it up as a mirror so that as we all check ourselves daily, even hourly if we need to, we will remember to ensure we are walking a sanctified life for and through Christ.

When we walk in such a way, we can be sure we will remain sanctified and that our light will surely shine brightly.

I encourage you all today, to take a deeper than usual look within, spend time on a life review and see what you need to change.

No-one knows the hour when Christ will knock on the door of our heart and say: *"It's time."*

Ensure your heart is cleansed, your love is kindled, and your lamp is trimmed. Be all you are meant to be in this life, and that

Preface

is much more than what you imagine. Be a light to the world because it needs you.

Whether you realize it or not, **you are special**, a one of a kind in the eyes of God; so, do not let life, people or circumstances tell you anything different - Kenzo

We Are All Sanctified **by** and **Through**
Christ when We Live a Sanctified Life

~ Kenzo Amariyo ~

Contents

Preface v

Who Is God? 1

The Lord's Love 5

Sanctification 11

Poems for Christians 17

    Thank You God 17

    Christ Is My Covering 19

    Angels Singing 21

    If the World Could See 22

    Chant Words of Praise 24

    Be Your Best 25

    Don't Fool with God 27

    God – I Have Let You Down 30

    Christ Crucified 32

    The Cleansing Blood 33

    Freed by God 35

    Don't Say Forgive Me 36

You Gave Me Life	37
Make Me a Light	40
In God I Will Trust	41
Approaching the Altar	42
Holy Thou Art (Not)	44
A Leader You May Be	45
Standing at the Table	46
Dressed in White	47
Holy, Holy, Holy	48
When Christ Looks	49
Crown and Glory	51
For the Wings of a Bird	53
If I Could Choose	54
I Prayed	58
The Gates of Love	60
Today May Be Your Day	62
On a Dark Winter's Night	65
We Never Know the Hour	68
It Was in the Night	70

Hallowed Be Thy Name	73
Broken	75
The Hermit	77
Jesus – The Sweetest One	80
You Are Worthy Lord	81
Wonderful	82
Adonai	84
We Give You Glory	85
Your Love is Heaven's Scent	87
Let the People See Your Light	88
The Chosen One	90
Glorify the Lord	91
You Renew My Strength	92
Open Our Eyes Lord	93
Make Me a Servant Lord	94
Glorify	96
It's All Upside Down	97
Merciful Father	99
He Came for You	100

Poems for Christians

In Christ We Live – In Christ We Die

Who Is God?

Chapter One

Who is God? What a question! Who can really explain that one?

For many, what or who God is will be a collection of bible verses that they have read or heard. For others, it will be what they were brought up to believe, for others still, it will be a vastly different answer.

Some believe God to be a person, a *'Him'* in the sky. Others focus on His essence as a spiritual being, as energy - universal energy, a divine source that is everywhere, and runs through and in all living things.

The word or term '*God*' means many things to many people, and I believe that we must all accept and respect the fact that what we as individuals believe to be God, is not necessarily what others believe to be God.

No-one can truly comprehend or fully explain that which is not truly comprehendible. When we try to explain what or who God is, we fail to explain the inexplicable spark of creation, the seed of life.

How can we, who are rooted in our physical body hope to explain something so spiritual?

As humans, we tend to need to find labels for everything, things cannot just *'be.'* We must label things and have some sort of explanation as to why it is what it is. We do this for us to understand and have a somewhat common knowledge of things so that we can communicate with each other without too much confusion. What a problem it would be if what you called a chair, I called a table!

Who Is God?

Who Is God? What an inviting question!

Surely this is a deep question that just begs you to delve deep into your own mind, you own heart, your own soul, a question which begs you to delve deep into your own psyche?

I encourage you to use this time to write down your own thoughts and ideas of who or what God is for you.

Whatever your concept of God is, I encourage you to permit it to permeate your soul, and to permit its essence to be the catalyst we all need to help us to change, grow, and evolve.

One thing we must all remember is this: If we are all made in His likeness, in His image, then we can all bring forth change.

We have all been blessed with the gift of creation all-be-it on a smaller scale, and we need to use and honour that gift responsibly and permit it to bring greatness into our own lives; and greatness may simply be the number of hearts we have touched in this lifetime.

For me, God is the source of all living things; we see God daily through people, animals, the earth, the sky. They are all reflections or aspects of God. If God created the heavens and the earth and all that is in it, then it makes sense that God is in all those things.

Give thanks daily to God and for God, and promise, just for today, you will behave in such a way that others will see God in you. You may be the only or last opportunity they have here on earth to find Him.

The Lord's Love

Chapter Two

"Love like God"

God so loved the world,
He gave His only son.
If I could love just half that much,
I would feel that I have won.

But feelings often are deeply hurt,
And people are full of regret.
Life goes by so swiftly,
And forgiveness we start to forget.

The Lord's Love

We forget the love we were given,
We forget the love Christ shows.
We become ensnared, in worldly cares,
Forgiveness!!! – I would rather cut off my nose!

But after all the bitterness,
And once we turn back to our Lord.
We start to hear His voice saying:
"Unforgiveness you shouldn't hoard.

For your heart was born in Heaven,
And all the Angels sing.
When you always choose forgiveness,
Over all negative things."

When we read about Jesus and his life, and all that He sacrificed and suffered, and the fact that He did it for love for us all; you cannot help but start to feel appreciation, humbleness, and gratitude.

We so often take His life for granted, we hear about His sacrifice so much, it is easy to start to feel or be blasé about it.

The Lord's Love

Often, because of broken trust in our close relationships, we find it difficult to believe in Christ's love and to accept His love. However, one thing we must remember is that God, our Lord, and the person(s) you have or had difficult feelings with are not the same.

If there is one thing, we can be sure of, it is that the Lord's love is never ending, it is not abusive, and He will never hurt us.

The Lord loves us with His heart and soul and we in return must learn to love not only Him but each other.

The more time we spend with someone, the more likely we are to become more like them. The more time we spend with Christ, the more likely we are to become like Him; and what a wonderful person to be like!

We all need to make that decision to be more Christ-like, to permit His love to flow to us and through us so we can be the change we need in our own life and the lives of those around us.

The Lord's Love

The world is a beautiful place and people are born as beautiful people, it is the journey and what is instilled within that makes the difference; good or bad.

It is so easy to become carried away with our own life, our own joys, and our own problems that we run the risk of becoming that Sunday saint. We remember God or Christ on Sunday morning whilst getting ready for Church, go to Church and be the good person we are expected to be, then go home and 'get on with life.'

God should be our life, He or It, the Divine Source, call it what you may, should be our life not a separate aspect of our life. God should be the driving force in all that we say and do.

How many times have we almost forgotten the love of Christ? Then something bad happens, and suddenly we find ourselves remembering Him and running to Him asking for help.

If we love Christ we will love Him daily, we will walk in love moment by

The Lord's Love

moment, not because we must or are expected to, but because our love and gratitude is so great that we realize that that is the least we can do for all He gave to us.

Loving God, loving Christ is not something we need to do, it is not something we should do or must do.

Loving God, loving Christ, is something we naturally do, because that love is so real it bubbles up within and flows naturally, just like the love we have for all the special people in our life.

Sanctification

Chapter Three

It is as we renew our minds that we can draw closer to The Divine and by drawing closer, we are then more able and enabled to do the work of God.

Romans 12:2

"Do not conform to the pattern of this world but be transformed by the renewing of your mind. Then you will be able to test and approve what God's will is-his good, pleasing, and perfect will."

Sanctification

To be sanctified by God is to be set apart; living a sanctified life is keeping yourself set apart for God's purpose and intentions. Sanctification not only comes through Christ, but it also comes from walking with and as Christ. We are given the gift of sanctification; in other words, we are washed clean and forgiven through grace. But this is only half of it, we then must choose to walk in a sanctified manner, we must keep ourselves sanctified and set apart for God. Sanctification is not a one-off deal, we are forgiven and cleansed for past sins, not for future ones. Continued sanctification requires us to choose to give up and let go of the things that displease God, the things that cause a divide between us and God. Sanctification happens within us when we choose to transform, or renew our minds, when we choose to feed it with more spiritual things. If we always fill our heads with negativity, we will eventually become negative, if we always fill our minds with divine things, we will eventually become as the divine; it may not happen quickly, it may not happen in this lifetime, but it will happen. When we realize and embody the idea of unlimited divine potential, we start to realize how much more we can be, how much more we can do to live a sanctified life.

1 Thessalonian's 5:23

"Now may the God of peace himself sanctify you completely and may your whole spirit and soul and body be kept blameless at the coming of our Lord Jesus Christ."

What a powerful verse! To be *sanctified* is not the same as to *be* sanctified. God sanctifies us by setting us apart (to be **sanctified**), then WE sanctify OURSELVES by setting us apart, (to *be* sanctified). The sanctification of God is the calling and receiving of His sanctification, the sanctification of our self, of our life, is the on-going process of being sanctified or Christ-Like. God sanctifies the un-sanctified AND the sanctified. We sanctify ourselves by becoming sanctified. One is receiving one is maintaining, to remain sanctified, one must maintain their lives, their minds, which in turn will govern their actions.

God is calling us closer, calling us to remember that we are made in God's image, we are not made any less, or anymore, but in God's image. What more could we ask for? we are co-creators and can create a beautiful life in God.

A servant's heart offers a life of giving, it is in that giving that they can and often are blessed with more than that which they require. First give, then receive, first plant then reap. The harvest is never cut before the wheat is planted, no more than the gifts of the Spirit can be gained before the planting of their seed. God has a plan, a plan for you,

Sanctification

a plan for me and a plan for us. The question is..............do you know what it is?

Poems for Christians

Chapter Four

"Thank You God"

Dear Lord and God,
From Heaven and Earth,
Today I thank you for my birth.
I thank you for my life and love,
The love which flows from you above.

I thank you for your son begotten,
For all my sins now forgotten.
I thank you for life ever-after,

Poems for Christians

Where we start a brand-new chapter.

I thank you for all those who care,
And pray for sinners everywhere.
I pray for those who live with hate,
Please get them through Heaven's gate.

I pray for those who just seem bad,
When really, they are mostly sad.
I pray for all the world you see,
Because you are so good to me.

Poems for Christians

"Christ Is My Covering"

Christ is my covering,
He holds me in His arms.
He keeps me safe each day,
Covered with His balm.

His blood is used as water,
To wash away my sin.
I know I am forgiven,
It draws me close to Him.

Take not His love for granted,
Do not sin and say, "oh well."
The only place you will go,
Is the fiery place called Hell.

We must all be responsible,
For what we say and do.
Even though it is automatic,
That Christ will forgive you.

We are all sanctified you know,
By His love and by the cross.

Poems for Christians

But that does not give permission,
To choose a life of dross.

We must choose the actions,
That show we are sincere.
Then we can fully rest,
And not live in such fear.

For Christ is always with us,
He is fair in all his ways.
But we too need to live,
For Christ for all our days.

"Angels Singing"

Angels singing around the throne,
Saints a praying, humbly prone.
People chanting words of praise,
Thanking God for all their days.

Christ adorned with heavenly crown,
Love – Compassion – all around.
What else could there possibly be,
More important than Holy Thee?

"If the World Could See"

If the world could see,
What I do see.
There would be no tears,
For you nor me.

There would be just Love,
Compassion, Hope.
For Divine Potential,
Brings much scope.

If the world could see,
His love so dear.
They would quickly drop,
All sin and fear.

They would open their hearts,
To God's supreme love.
They would sense his forgiveness,
Straight from above.

If the world could see,
His arms open wide.

Poems for Christians

*They would change their ways,
No need to hide.*

*The peace of God,
Would fill their heart.
In a loving relationship,
That would never part.*

"Chant Words of Praise"

Chant the words of praise each day,
Keep the devil far away.
Keep your thoughts pure and clean,
Then your halo will be seen.

Glory, glory Angel's voices,
Singing praises for your choices.
Singing, dancing cheering on,
Closer to the throne you have gone.

Chant the words of praise each day,
Positioned prone in a humble way.
Praise and glory will fill your heart,
Sanctification will surely start.

The key is not to just receive,
That idea you must leave.
A relationship of love takes two,
That is surely Christ and YOU.

"Be Your Best"

Be the best that you can be,
Do not get caught up with sin and see.
See how Christ honours your ways,
His love abiding all your days.

Do not sin and say, "all is forgiven,
Christ accepts my sin forbidden.
Christ just loves me as I am,"
With this mistake you are surely damned.

Sanctified in Christ we be,
Though not a ticket to sin, you see.
Take responsibility for choices,
Do not listen to the devils' voices.

He says: "do not change, stay as you are,
You are accepted like a shining star.
Hold un-forgiveness, hate, and spite,
God accepts you; He sees your light.

Keep on sinning, do not change your ways,
There is plenty of time, plenty of days.

Poems for Christians

Do not trim your lamp, or heart,
Christ has loved you from the start."

Whilst true this is, upon one level,
Do not be tricked by the devil.
For Christ expects us all to change,
For we can grow and loose the reins.

For babes in Christ we cannot stay,
An adult we must become one day.
Choose to lose that self so low,
Be assured of where you will go.

Be the image and Christ's reflection,
Going in the right direction.
Then in time you will surely be,
Living with Christ - you and me.

"Don't Fool with God"

Don't fool with God,
He is not your brother.
He is not your sister,
Significant other.

He knows your heart,
He sees your sin.
You need forgiveness,
So let Him in.

We have all fallen short,
We have all needed grace.
It seems to be,
The human race.

We have all lost touch,
Of our God Divine.
We take things for granted,
What is yours is mine.

We search in the world,
For Heavenly love.

Poems for Christians

Not realizing,
That it comes from above.

It comes from a source,
We cannot see.
A loving Father,
He wants to be.

Don't fool with God,
It is not very smart.
He is looking within,
At your very heart.

He sees every breath,
Whether in or out.
He knows if you love Him,
Of that there is no doubt.

He is looking for people,
Whose love is true.
Those are the ones,
Who will make it through.

Those are the ones,

Who will sit at His throne.
Singing, dancing,
Praying prone.

Don't fool with God,
He is beginning and end.
Open your heart,
And His love He will send.

"God – I have Let You Down"

Dear God, I have gone and let you down,
For this I am sure there will be no crown.
I have done the things you loath the most,
I have grieved you, and the Holy Ghost.

Please help me change the way I am,
I know with you I surely can.
I know you will be my strength and power,
You will see me through, every hour.

I ask again forgiveness please,
I pray sincerely on my knees.
Help me walk your ways so pure,
Then I can reach Heaven's door.

I am weak, I am stupid, without you,
Lust and greed are what I do.
I need you more and more each day,
Help me please in every way.

I want to make you oh so proud,
So that you shout this from the clouds:

Poems for Christians

*"Hallelujah – he has come back home,
No longer lost, no need to roam."*

*Then proud I will feel, to be your son,
Knowing you are the only one.
To set me free and heal my pain,
Until that day we meet again.*

"Christ Crucified"

They hung Him on a cross so high,
The air was filled with people's cries.
They crucified the Son of God,
Such sinful land, they all trod.

They took His clothes, they took His lot,
But Christ my Lord, is not forgot.
He rose again, in all His glory,
This is the truth, and not a story.

He rose again, all pure and light,
He gave us hope, on a dark, dark night.
He showed the way, like a twinkling star,
Love and compassion – He raised the bar.

He is our example, of how we should live,
With love and compassion, willingness to give.
All we need, is faith in our heart,
And from the Lord, we will never part.

"The Cleansing Blood"

The blood of Christ, washes clean,
All our sin, all that is mean.
It purifies us, just like gold,
It buffs us up, makes us feel bold.

The dross is gone, alive we be,
But we must now, walk as free.
So do not return, to sin's dark way,
Upon this path, you must surely stay.

Your worldly side, has been forgiven,
By the devil, be not driven.
He will drive you back, to sin and dust,
Where you will drown, within your lust.

The lust of flesh, and worldly things,
Pain and suffering, it surely brings.
But Christ will bring you, home again,
Then you will never, be the same.

Be not broken, by the rock,
Even if your friends do mock.

Poems for Christians

Know the truth, as time goes by,
The blood of Christ is not a lie.

Let him wash you, once again,
Let your tears, fall just like rain.
Feel forgiveness, in your heart,
A life with Christ, you will surely start.

"Freed by God"

I met with God, and asked today,
That he would take, my sins away.
He said He would, so not to worry,
Like little mice, they all would scurry.

But I would have to make a promise,
That from today, I would be honest.
That I would stop, hiding sins of flesh,
And realize, it is just a mesh.

A nasty mesh, of bondage and pain,
And from such things, I must refrain.
That I can sit, with God above,
Resting in, His arms of love.

"Don't Say Forgive Me"

Don't say "forgive me," then do it again,
From such things you, must refrain.
How can you look me, in the eye?
And say, "I'm sorry," and start to cry.

Then tomorrow, you do the same,
And yet again, shed tears like rain.
"I am sorry," means you have fallen short,
Of your sins, you have been caught.

Clean your act, and cleanse your heart,
If you do not want us, to ever part.
I am not a fool, I see all things,
To the Altar, you must bring.

All those parts, that need me most,
But do not insult, the Holy Ghost.
By going back, to a sinner's bed,
Cleanse your heart, not just your head.

"You Gave Me Life"

You gave me life,
When I was down.
You heard my cry,
No-one around.

You lifted me up,
From torment and pain.
And now,
I will never be the same.

You took my sadness,
You took my shame.
You gave me hope,
And love again.

You did what no-one,
Else could do.
You opened my eyes,
Now I see you.

You are my life,
You are my love.

You are my everything,
From above.

You are my saviour,
When times get tough.
You calm my ocean,
When it gets rough.

You dry my tears,
You heal my heart.
From you my Lord,
I will not depart.

You are my anchor,
In the storm.
You are my healer,
When I am worn.

You gave me life,
Of that, I am sure.
So go ahead,
And make me pure.

For all I want,

*Is life with you.
To reflect your light,
In all I do.*

"Make Me a Light"

Make me a light, to show the way,
So those who need you, day by day.
Can see you deep, inside my heart,
And from your path, will not depart.

Make me a light, bright and strong,
Then all those people, who have done wrong.
Will find forgiveness, for all they did,
Guilt and shame, they will be rid.

Make me a light, as bright as the sun,
Then all the people, will start to run.
As fast as they can, to your Holy altar,
Seeking forgiveness, pledging to not falter.

Make me a light, to show the way,
Until the end, when I must say.
Goodbye.

"In God I Will Trust"

Job was a man, with torment and pain,
I am sure he cried, tears like rain.
I am sure he doubted, God at times,
And such doubting, is no crime.

We all have times, when doubt creeps in,
And of this doubt, there is no sin.
We all have times, when faith has gone,
So do not worry, God's will be done.

Spend quiet times, with God each day,
And soon you will chase, the blues away.
You will feel refreshed, and faith will grow,
You are not forgotten, do you know?

The hardest times, He holds your hands,
And safely guides you, through the land.
And when you hurt, and feel fear too,
Those are the times, He carries you.

"Approaching the Altar"

You make your way,
To God's pure altar.
With your steps,
You fail to falter.

But in your heart,
A different story.
Your un-forgiveness,
Brings no glory.

You sing, you pray,
You raise your hands.
Whilst held so tight,
By sins gold band.

Before you reach,
The Altar, please.
Put down your gifts,
On bended knees.

Seek forgiveness,

Poems for Christians

From God first.
Then go out,
And find the worst.

All those you hate,
Secretly despise.
Ask them for forgiveness,
That would be wise.

Then come again,
To God's pure table.
Now you are cleansed,
You are more able.

To offer gifts,
Of sacrifice.
I do believe,
This is most wise.

"Holy Thou Art (Not)"

Holy thou art,
Amongst Christian friends.
Little do they know,
How much your heart does lend.

It lends itself to sin,
Of such abominable sort.
It will not be too long now,
Before you are finally caught.

"A Leader You May Be"

A leader you may be,
Of Heaven and all God's ways.
But your sin has you numbered,
It is only a matter of days.

The day of reckoning will stink,
And Hell on earth let loose.
You will find yourself a hanging,
By your own handmade noose.

"Standing at the Table"

You are standing at the table,
A leader of the church.
About to take communion,
For all its heavenly worth.

But in your heart, you harbour,
Unforgiveness, to your brother.
To another leader,
And, to your mother.

Hypocrisy is not ok,
It is not a pleasant smell.
Come clean your heart, first my dear,
Or you may be going to hell.

"Dressed in White"

Dressed in white,
He took my hands.
Bound together,
By spiritual bands.

He placed a crown,
Upon my head.
Assuring me,
I was not dead.

He said that life,
Does not stand still.
And once I pass,
The Holy Hill.

I will reach a place,
I thought I would never.
Where I would remain,
For ever and ever.

"Holy, Holy, Holy"

Holy, Holy, Holy,
Is our God Almighty.
All of Heaven and earth,
Will praise His worthy name.

Angels singing sweetly,
Trumpets playing loudly.
Cymbals resounding endlessly,
Praising His worthy name.

Holy, Holy, Holy,
When will we start to see?
We must grow within,
And praise His worthy name.

Poems for Christians

"When Christ Looks"

When Christ looks down,
What does He see?
What does He see,
When He looks at you and me?

Does He see the hate?
Does He see the pain?
Does He see our heart,
Breaking again?

When Christ looks down,
He sees it all.
He sees us fly,
And when we fall.

He sees our sin,
He sees our love.
He intercedes,
From far above.

He sees us soar,
On eagle's wings.

Poems for Christians

He sees our actions,
So many things.

He sees us drop,
Like a sparrow, so small.
He sees our tears,
When they fall.

He sees so much,
Too much to mention.
He sees our motives,
And intentions.

He knows which ones,
Walk in His way.
He is here to help,
Do not lose your way.

He is full of love,
A sincere heart.
And from that,
Only fools would part.

Poems for Christians

"Crown and Glory"

Crown and glory,
Is the story,
Behind our risen Lord.

Many failing,
Others sailing,
Never getting bored.

Children chatter,
Old one's natter,
Talking of our Saviour.

Some begin,
To understand,
The need to change behaviour.

New wine,
Must have new skin,
We know, to keep it fresh.

The same goes,

Poems for Christians

For body and soul,
As change removes the mesh.

In time,
All is understood,
We comprehend and grow.

That is the time,
When wisdom comes,
And we finally do not let go.

"For the Wings of a Bird"

Oh, for the wings of a bird,
Where I could soar the sky.
Where I could draw so close,
To you and ask you why?

Oh, for the wings of a bird,
I could escape my pain.
I could fly high,
And be in your arms again.

"If I Could Choose"

If I could choose, to change my life,
I would change it, from today.
I would change the way, I treat my wife,
On any given day.

I would change, my grumpy attitude,
I would change, my sulky soul.
My anger, I would surely bury,
Deep within a hole.

I would change, my personality,
Then I would be, much less mean.
I would ask to be, more like Christ,
Then goodness could be seen.

Instead of hate, love would shine.
Within my heart, and eyes.
But now, I am ashamed,
For everyone just cries.

I hate myself, for being me,
Dear God, please make be love.

Poems for Christians

Then suddenly, I hear a voice,
It comes from up above.

The voice it says, in words of love,
"My dearest, and my brother.
Believe me, when I say you can,
Change into another.

You are all born, with seeds of Christ,
A planted, in your hearts.
You only need, to water them,
And then, the magic starts.

You will see, that from the damp and dark,
A small seed does start to sprout.
And as it grows, and spreads itself,
It pushes dark weeds out.

For love will always conquer,
It is the way I made your heart.
All you must do, my friend,
Is commit to a brand-new start.

Commit yourself unto my ways,

Poems for Christians

And never start to falter.
Bring all your dross, that you do have,
And leave it at my Altar.

Once let go, do not take it back,
Do not go back to your old life.
But start a fresh, and be the man,
I chose for your dear wife.

You cannot beat her, it is just not right,
For that you will repent.
And if you do not, rest assured,
Your path will be Hell bent.

Forgiveness starts with you, and me,
And then, with your dear mother.
Then individually ask,
Forgiveness from the other.

Be humble, and be on your knees,
Come pray to me each day.
And I will keep you, from all harm,
And help you on your way.

But listen close, it is not a path,
That you should lightly tread.
But walk in faith, and know,
Your sins are on your head.

Now take responsibility,
For all you say and do.
Then forgiveness, you will have,
And my love will follow you."

"I Prayed"

I prayed to my dear Lord today,
That He would heal my heart.
I prayed that he would cherish me,
And never let us part.

I prayed that all things, good and fine,
Would flow down from above.
I prayed sweet words would leave my lips,
On the wings of a dove.

I prayed that only goodness,
Would reside within my heart.
That this would be the very day,
My Christ-like life would start.

He said, "My child do not worry,
I see your heart and mind.
I hear your prayers daily,
I see you are so kind.

I see your love sweet flowing,
Like honey from a tree.

Poems for Christians

I know your love is true,
That is not hard to see.

Because your heart is pure,
In everything you do.
Rest assured, my love will shine,
Forever, through-out you."

"The Gates of Love"

I threw the gates wide open,
Rushed through, to find my love.
I knew He would be waiting,
He would come on wings of a dove.

My heart feels light and airy,
I hear whispers in my ear.
I feel His touch, so gentle,
Can you not feel it, my dear?

His love is never-ending,
It reaches your very core.
When I spend much time, with Him,
My worries are no more.

For all that overwhelms me,
Suddenly disappears.
I seem to gain right back,
Many lost years.

I suddenly forget,
All the things that had me down.

Poems for Christians

He truly is the best,
He who wears that crown.

"Today May Be Your Day"

If you do not know my God,
Today may be your day.
I see your pain a written,
On your face in many ways.

I want you to know now,
He is always there for you.
He knows you are hurting,
He will help, if you want Him to.

He cares so much more,
More than you could even know.
Even though you do not believe,
Perhaps give Him ago.

There is nothing you can lose,
By falling at His feet.
And calling out to Him,
"Dear Father let us meet.

Please come and show your presence,
Let me feel your love so great.

Poems for Christians

That I may have your blessings,
Before it is too late.

I am sick and dying slowly,
With pain and torment too.
There is nothing in the world,
So now I turn to you.

I hope you really hear me,
Because I am praying, from my heart.
I wish I had known you sooner,
Known you from the start.

My life would have been different,
My choices not so grim.
Hopefully, it is not too late,
Too late to let you in.

On deaths door, I am praying,
That a saviour will save my day.
And if that is not possible,
Then carry me away.

Carry me away,

To a place where I find rest.
Where I can this very day,
Lay gently, on your chest.

And as I lay there quietly,
Please let both your loving arms.
Wrap right around by being,
Bringing love and a welcome calm."

"On a Dark Winter's Night"

Lost on a boat,
On a dark winters night.
Terrified of the outcome,
Feeling real fright.

Worried about dying,
Where I may be.
Scaring all hope,
Right out of me.

But far in the distance,
I see a light.
It seems so small,
But very bright.

And then I feel,
The light within.
And suddenly,
A voice says: "Do not give in.

Do not let your worries,
Do not let your strife.

Poems for Christians

Take away hope,
Love and life.

Do not let the problems,
That seem so grotesque.
Take away faith,
And happiness.

Fix your gaze,
On that small, still light.
Let it grow,
And become so bright.

Draw it closer,
And you will see.
That bright light,
Is truly me.

I am always here,
I am never there.
Exercise faith,
If you dare.

And you will see,

Poems for Christians

The water still.
And every mountain,
Become, just a hill.

For I am your God,
The magician of life.
I can make the sun shine,
I can take away strife.

But most of you pray,
And ask me for help.
Then keep hanging on,
Like a dog's whelp.

You must let it go,
You must try and trust.
That is not a choice,
That is a must.

If you do not give me,
The thing you despise.
How on earth can you learn,
Or ever, be wise?

"We Never Know the Hour"

Flying around the corner,
It came at such a speed.
Forty miles per hour,
He did not seem to heed.

Right out of control,
And through the iron gate.
The car went a flying,
It was already, too late.

There he lay, motionless,
His body already dying.
Everyone could see,
Everyone was crying.

Panic, panic everywhere,
Nothing could be done.
Twenty-four and suddenly,
All his life was gone.

Let us take great heed,
Ensuring every day.

Poems for Christians

We keep alert and vigilant,
And walk in Heaven's way.

We never know our hour,
We never know our day.
Or when our time is over,
And we are suddenly whisked away.

"It Was in the Night"

It was in the night,
When sun had set,
And heavy clouds hung low.

When all around,
Seemed dark and grey,
To the graveyard I did go.

I went to see,
My long-lost love,
To speak awhile and say.

How much there missed,
And send a kiss,
Until another day.

At first, I stood,
And tears did flood,
The headstone at my feet.

Then to my knees,
I gently fell,

Poems for Christians

And asked when we would meet.

The pain was great,
For Heaven's sake,
When will this void close tightly?

I cannot bear,
The pain no more,
I prayed to the Almighty.

"What have you done?
Where has he gone?
My love and my dear friend.

With broken dreams,
And inner screams,
Can I make it to the end?"

Then up I got,
And home I trot,
In wind and rain and cold.

The only thoughts,
Upon my mind,

Poems for Christians

Was that I must be bold.

People die,
All the time,
Of that, we have no say.

I must move on,
With my life,
And take it day by day.

"Hallowed Be Thy Name"

Our Father who art in Heaven,
Hallowed, be thy name.
We thank you for your grace,
We will never be the same.

You rescued us from hell,
We were living it here on earth.
Trapped and chained in cycles,
That started from our birth.

Generational curses,
Holding families bound tight.
Never having freedom,
Never seeing light.

But now we turn a leaf,
We start a brand-new day.
Because all chains are broken,
In every single way.

So now the family's free,
Like a tree beside still waters.

Poems for Christians

It is not just us you have freed,
But sisters, brothers, daughters.

So today, we are rejoicing,
And praising your worthy name.
Because of you dear God,
We no longer wear a chain.

"Broken"

I look into the mirror,
I did not like what I could see.
I saw a broken body,
It was certainly not me.

I have always been so active,
Living life to the full.
This person in the mirror,
Is looking very dull.

She cannot run or walk,
She cannot jump and praise.
She cannot comprehend,
Many of God's ways.

She cannot cook and clean,
She cannot go to work.
But she does not sit and moan,
She sees it as a perk.

But upon deep reflection,
I recognize the smile.

I start to hear her words,
She goes that extra mile.

I start to see how 'broken,'
Is ministering to others.
I start to see the change,
In sisters and in brothers.

So now, I look again,
And see it is truly me.
On a different path,
Than what I used to be.

But in all things, there are blessings,
I had to look to see.
And one day, the reasoning,
Will be revealed to me.

Until that day arrives,
I thank God for who I am.
Broken on the outside,
But gentle as a lamb.

"The Hermit"

The Hermit lives,
Her life in stillness.
Praising God,
Through health and illness.

Thankful for bread,
And water given.
To lust and greed,
She is never driven.

Her humble abode,
Is simple and neat.
Somewhere to sleep,
Somewhere to eat.

She has all her needs,
Day after day.
Humbly praying,
After God's ways.

Hardly seen,
And hardly heard.

Some say – "She is useless"
That is absurd.

The things of God,
Spring from the heart.
They keep you close,
Then you do not part.

The Hermit wears,
An invisible crown.
Praying for all,
That they do not drown.

That they do not drown,
In sorrows and lust.
And will surely reach Heaven,
And in that we must trust.

So always give thanks,
For the Hermit who prays.
Who does not say much,
All her days.

Pray that God's strength,

Poems for Christians

Would keep her real strong.
That her health would be good,
And her years very long.

"Jesus – The Sweetest One"

Jesus,
You are the sweetest one.
You are always here,
When all are gone.

You are by my side,
Both day and night.
You take the bad,
And make it right.

Jesus,
There is none like you.
You wipe my tears,
When I am blue.

You are like fresh honey,
On lips when dry,
You catch my tears,
Each time I cry.

"You Are Worthy Lord"

You are worthy of worship,
You are worthy of praise.
I lift my voice towards Heaven,
My arms I do raise.

You are worthy of trust,
You are worth of love.
With all my heart,
I pray to you above.

My Lord,
What a wonder you certainly are.
You shine so brightly.
You are the Morning Star,

Many do not know you,
How fortunate am I!
Walking with you,
Until the day I die.

"Wonderful"

They call Him Wonderful,
They call Him Saviour.
He watches over us,
Sees our behaviour.

He sees our hearts,
He knows each hair.
He loves us dearly,
He really cares.

My first true love,
He will be my last.
We have walked together,
He knows my past.

No-one can love me,
Like He loves me.
No-one can bring,
My heart so much glee.

He is my smile,
My reason for living.

Poems for Christians

He is all He could be,
Never short on giving.

He gives Himself,
With totality.
What more in life,
Could there possibly be?

The beginning and the end,
And all in between.
And never has love,
Like His been seen.

I am head over heels,
And falling fast.
My love for Him,
Will surely last.

"Adonai"

Adonai, Adonai,
I call from despair.
Help me, help me,
Bring release from this snare.

Ensnared in sin,
And lustful ways.
Sick and diseased,
With limited days.

Adonai, Adonai,
Show me your face.
Forgive me please,
Show me your grace.

A sinner am I,
Not worthy in your sight.
But pleading still,
Please show me your light.

"We Give You Glory"

Dear Lord,

We thank you,
For all you have done.
You truly are,
The special one.

And for that,
We give you glory and praise.
Not just today,
But for all our days.

Your glory and grace,
Falls like summer rain.
Quenching our thirst,
Making us worthy again.

We give you glory Lord,
For all that you have given.
I pray, by you,
I will surely be driven.

Poems for Christians

We give you glory Lord,
We give you praise.
We will worship you,
For all our days.

"Your Love is Heaven's Scent"

Above the world,
And all the wise.
You stand so strong,
You took the prize.

You gave yourself,
To wolves and hounds.
Now you stand,
On Holy ground.

As Lord of Lords,
And King of Kings,
All you touch,
Becomes beautiful things.

You are the power,
You are our strength.
Your love fills the earth,
It is Heaven's scent.

"Let the People See Your Light"

Praise the Father,
Praise the Lord,
Praise the loving Holy Ghost.

Worship the trinity,
Bow in honour,
Acknowledge Heaven's Holy Host.

Voices singing,
Bells a ringing,
Praise and worship everywhere.

Angel's dancing,
Beasts a prancing,
Worshipping without a care.

Glory, Glory,
Hallelujah,
Energy is building high.

People falling,
Voices calling,

Poems for Christians

Worshiping day and night.

Spread the word,
Let God be heard,
Let the people see your light.

"The Chosen One"

Mary was God's chosen one,
In her He did delight.
He saw that she was worthy,
To bring the world His light.

He knew she would not falter,
With Joseph by her side.
Impregnated by His Spirit,
And that she could not hide.

It was a dangerous path,
That she did undertake.
But faith and love for God,
Made her put her life at stake.

We must all remember,
That God knows what is best.
And we will always have,
Our faith put to the test.

"Glorify the Lord"

Glorify the Lord of Heaven,
Love, compassion from above.
Cleansed and saved, by His presence,
Purified by His blood.

If we truly know our Saviour,
If we truly feel His love.
Surely, we would make good choices,
Cleanse our heart, like His above?

If we truly know our Lord,
If He calls us by our name.
Surely, we would, with eyes wide open,
Walk the path with love not shame?

Glorify the Lord of Heaven,
Thank Him daily for His grace.
Show Him gratitude, through actions,
Loving all the human race.

"You Renew My Strength"

You renew my strength, O Lord,
You quench my inner thirst.
My soul longs for you, each day,
You are my last love, and my first.

You are my friend, and my lover,
You are my Saviour, and my King.
From the very day we met,
You caused my heart to sing.

When I awake up every morning,
I just want to see your face.
I want to feel your presence,
No one can take your place.

My first, my last, my everything,
My heart, and soul, for you.
I will trust you Lord, in everything,
In everything I do.

"Open Our Eyes Lord"

Open our eyes Lord,
That we can see your love.
That we can feel, the sacrifice,
Made from Heaven above.

No one has loved me more Lord,
In the way that you do.
Unconditional, and forgiving,
Grace received from you.

Our relationship is serious,
It is built on love and trust.
And one day, in the future Lord,
Into your arms I will rush.

"Make Me a Servant Lord"

Make me a servant Lord,
Strong instead of weak.
Help me to guide,
All those who feel meek.

Help me to strengthen,
Others and I, too.
Help me to show love,
In all I say and do.

Make me a servant Lord,
That reflects the perfect you.
Enlarge my heart Lord,
That I may be humble in all I do.

Let me be a bright light,
For others to swiftly follow.
Let me pour in love,
In those who feel so hollow.

Make me a servant Lord,
I will wipe away their tears.

Poems for Christians

I will hold people gently,
All those broken for years.

I will serve Lord, and I will give,
For the rest of my days.
I will follow you forever,
And walk in your ways.

Make me a servant Lord.

"Glorify"

I will glorify your name Lord,
Each day I walk this earth.
Remembering your love,
And the reason for my birth.

I will lift your name up high Lord,
By all I say and do.
I will sacrifice my life,
Simply because it is you.

I will glorify your name Lord,
In speech and actions pure.
I will carry my own cross,
The pain I will endure.

You gave me your begotten son,
What more could you give?
And because of your sacrifice,
For you only, I will live.

Poems for Christians

"It's All Upside Down"

Lord, the world seems upside down,
We do not know what to do.
I guess the only thing,
Is to put our trust in you.

What once was wrong is now called right,
And right is now called bad.
We need your help Lord in the world,
It seems like all is mad.

They lie, they cheat, bad things they say,
They steal and keep it hidden.
They teach our children all things wrong,
And brag about things forbidden.

They rob our friends, they do not mind,
They rob our parents too.
There is no doubt, that given the chance,
They would rob all things from you.

We know you can turn things around,
And change the hearts of men.

Poems for Christians

I guess the question is not how,
I guess the questions – when?

Time is short, and night draws in,
And clouds form overhead.
I pray your will be done my Lord,
Each night before my bed.

"Merciful Father"

Merciful Father,
I fall at your feet.
Completely broken,
I cannot help but weep.

Like a sheep that is lost,
A lamb for the slaughter.
Forgive me Father,
It is me, your daughter.

I am lost, I am weary,
I am crushed to the bone.
Emotionally drained,
A heart of stone.

Merciful Father,
Please hold me today.
That I may find grace,
And walk in your way.

"He Came for You"

Dear God,

I know you hear my prayer,
I know you see all things.
Today I pray for all the world,
For good things that you would bring.

So many people in the world,
That still do not know of you.
It really breaks my heart dear Lord,
Because of what you do.

You take us each by the hand,
And lead us to your throne.
Many reach there thankfully,
Whilst others stop and moan.

For me, I give thanks each day,
I know what I have been given.
I know the grace you have shown me Lord,
And that is why I am truly driven.

Poems for Christians

I am driven to share your wonders,
Your love, and your salvation.
I am driven to share your grace,
And encourage conversation.

And if you read this poem today,
No matter what you do.
He gave His life for all,
And that my dear, means YOU!

Thank You for Purchasing this Book

Other Books by Kenzo

Micro-Poetry

Poems of Childhood Pain

Poems for Loved Ones

Spiritual Healing

True Ghost Stories

Urinalysis, Alkalinity & Well-Being

The Effects of Shamanic Healing & Other Healing Practices on General Well-Being